MY FIRST BOOK ABOUT

NEW JERSEY

by Carole Marsh

This activity book has material which correlates with the New Jersey Core Curriculum Content Standards. At every opportunity, we have tried to relate information to the History and Social Science, English, Science, Math, Civics, Economics, and Computer Technology CCCS directives. For additional information, go to our websites: **www.newjerseyexperience.com** or **www.gallopade.com**.

Gallopade is proud to be a member of these educational organizations and associations:

The New Jersey Experience Series

The New Jersey Experience Paperback Book!

My First Pocket Guide to New Jersey!

The Big New Jersey Reproducible Activity Book

The New Jersey Coloring Book!

My First Book About New Jersey!

New Jersey "Jography!": A Fun Run Through Our State

New Jersey Jeopardy: Answers & Questions About Our State

The New Jersey Experience! Sticker Pack

The New Jersey Experience! Poster/Map

Discover New Jersey CD-ROM

New Jersey "GEO" Bingo Game

New Jersey "HISTO" Bingo Game

A Word... From the Author

Do you know when I think children should start learning about their very own state? When they're born! After all, even when you're a little baby, this is your state too! This is where you were born. Even if you move away, this will always be your "home state." And if you were not born here, but moved here—this is still your state as long as you live here.

We know people love their country. Most people are very patriotic. We fly the U.S. flag. We go to Fourth of July parades. But most people also love their state. Our state is like a mini-country to us. We care about its places and people and history and flowers and birds.

As a child, we learn about our little corner of the world. Our room. Our home. Our yard. Our street. Our neighborhood. Our town. Even our county.

But very soon, we realize that we are part of a group of neighbor towns that make up our great state! Our newspaper carries stories about our state. The TV news is about happenings in our state. Our state's sports teams are our favorites. We are proud of our state's main tourist attractions.

From a very young age, we are aware that we are a part of our state. This is where our parents pay taxes and vote and where we go to school. BUT, we usually do not get to study about our state until we are in school for a few years!

So, this book is an introduction to our great state. It's just for you right now. Why wait to learn about your very own state? It's an exciting place and reading about it now will give you a head start for that time when you "officially" study our state history! Enjoy,

Carole Marsh

New Jersey
Let's Have Words!

Make as many words as you can from the letters in the words:

THE GARDEN STATE!

_____   _____   _____

_____   _____   _____

_____   _____   _____

_____   _____   _____

_____   _____   _____

_____   _____   _____

_____   _____   _____

_____   _____   _____

_____   _____   _____

_____   _____   _____

_____   _____   _____

_____   _____   _____

New Jersey
Nickname

New Jersey has several nicknames. It is called the Garden State, the Clam State, and the Pathway of Revolution.

What other nicknames would suit our state and why?

_____

_____

_____

_____

_____

What nicknames would suit your town or your school?

_____

_____

_____

_____

_____

What's your nickname?

Nick.

New Jersey
How BIG is Our State?

Our state is the 5th smallest in the U.S. It is made up of 8,215 square miles (21,277 square kilometers).

Can you answer the following questions?

1. How many states are there in the United States?

_____

2. This many states are smaller than our state:

_____

3. This many states are larger than our state:

_____

4. One mile = 5,280 _____ _____ _____ _____

     HINT:

5. Draw a picture of a "square" mile below:

BIGFOOT WAS HERE!

New Jersey
People

A state is not just towns and mountains and rivers. A state is its people! The really important people in a state are not famous. You may know them—they may be your mom, your dad, or your teacher. The average, everyday person is the one who makes the state a good state. How? By working hard, by paying taxes, by voting, and by helping New Jersey children grow up to be good state citizens!

Match these New Jersey people with their accomplishment.

1. Kenneth Gibson

2. Bill Bradley

3. Frank Sinatra

4. Clara Barton

5. Judy Blume

6. Mary Mapes Dodge

7. Thomas Edison

8. Albert Einstein

9. Grover Cleveland

10. Edwin "Buzz" Aldrin

A. started first New Jersey public school
B. Author of *Superfudge*
C. invented electric light, and phonograph
D. first African-American mayor of Newark
E. author of *Hans Brinker, or, The Silver Skates*
F. 2nd man ever to walk on the moon
G. basketball player turned politician
H. 22nd and 24th U.S. president
I. scientist famous for the theory of relativity
J. "Old Blue Eyes," or "Chairman of the Board"

ANSWERS: 1.D 2.G 3.J 4.A 5.B 6.E 7.C 8.I 9.H 10.F

New Jersey
Gazetteer

A gazetteer is a list of places. Use the word bank to complete the names of some of these famous places in our state:

1. _ _ _ _ _ _ _ _ CITY

2. THE _ _ _ _ _ WALK

3. PINE _ _ _ _ _ _ _

4. _ _ _ _ _ _ _ _ _ _ MOUNTAINS

5. _ _ _ _ TON

6. _ _ _ _ MAY

7. _ _ _ _ _ _ _ _ RIVER

8. NEW JERSEY _ _ _ _ _ _ _ _

9. _ _ _ _ _ _ SHORE

10. _ _ _ _ _ _

WORD BANK

Cape May
Delaware River
New Jersey Turnpike
Jersey Shore
Newark

The Boardwalk
Pine Barrens
Kittatinny Mountains
Atlantic City
Trenton

ANSWERS: 1. Atlantic City 2. The Boardwalk 3. Pine Barrens 4. Kittatinny Mountains 5. Trenton 6. Cape May 7. Delaware River 8. New Jersey Turnpike 9. Jersey Shore 10. Newark

New Jersey
Neighbors

No person or state lives alone. You have neighbors where you live. Sometimes they may be right next door. Other times, they may be way down the road. You live in the same neighborhood and are interested in what goes on there.

You have neighbors at school. The children who sit in front, beside, or behind you are your neighbors. You may share books. You might borrow a pencil. They might ask you to move so they can see the board better.

We have a lot in common with our state neighbors. Some of our land is alike. We share some history. We care about our part of the country. We share borders. Some of our people go there; some of their people come here. Most of the time we get along with our state neighbors. Even when we argue or disagree, it is a good idea for both of us to work it out. After all, states are not like people—they can't move away!

Use the color key to color New Jersey and its neighbors.

Color Key:

New Jersey–blue
New York–green
Pennsylvania–red
Delaware–orange

New Jersey
Highs and Lows

The highest point in New Jersey is High Point. High Point lies in Sussex county in northern New Jersey. At the summit, there is a 240 feet (73 meters) tall monument which was built in 1930.

Draw a picture of High Point.

The lowest point in New Jersey is where the Jersey Shore meets the Atlantic ocean, at sea level.

Draw a picture of the Jersey Shore.

New Jersey
Old Man River

New Jersey has many great rivers. Rivers give us water for our crops. Rivers are also water "highways." On these water highways travel crops, manufactured goods, people, and many other things—including children in tire tubes!

Here are some of New Jersey's most important rivers:

- Hudson
- Maurice
- Great Egg Harbor
- Delaware
- Passaic
- Musconetcong
- Mullica
- Toms
- Raritan
- Hackensack

Draw someone "tubing" down a New Jersey River!

New Jersey
Weather ... Or Not!

What kind of climate does our state have?

New Jersey has weather that is similar to other states on the eastern seaboard. New Jersey can have very hot and very cold weather. The state's average rainfall is usually between 40 and 50 inches (100-125 centimeters). Although located on the ocean, winds from the west usually determine New Jersey's weather.

You might think adults talk about the weather a lot. But our state's weather is very important to us. Crops need water and sunshine. Weather can affect the tourist industry. Good weather can mean more money for our state. Bad weather can cause problems that cost money.

ACTIVITY: Do you watch the nightly news at your house? If you do, you might see the weather report. Tonight, tune in the weather report. The reporter often talks about our state's regions, cities and towns, and our neighboring states. Watching the weather report is a great way to learn about our state. It also helps you know what to wear to school tomorrow!

What is the weather outside now? Draw a picture.

New Jersey
Indian Tribes

The Leni-Lenape Indians, which means "genuine people" or "original people," lived in New Jersey before the first Europeans settled there. Colonists later called them the "Delaware" because many of the Native Americans lived along the Delaware River.

Help Maize find her way through the maize (corn) field maze to her hut made of saplings!

Start

Finish

New Jersey
Website Page

Here is a website you can go to and learn more about New Jersey: **www.state.nj.us**

Design your own state website page on the computer screen below.

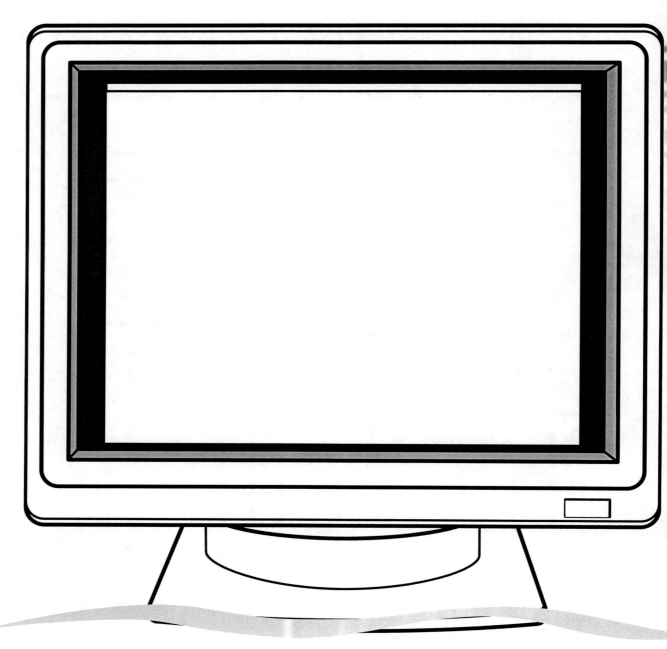

Can you dig Archaeology?

New Jersey's dinosaur is the Hadrosaurus. Color the Hadrosaurus below.

State Animal

In 1977, Governor Brendan T. Byrne signed a law making the horse the official state animal of New Jersey. The governor signed the law at the farm and horse show in Augusta. The United States Equestrian Team is headquartered in New Jersey.

Color the horse below.

New Jersey
Spelling Bee!

What's All The Buzz About?

Here are some words related to New Jersey. See if you can find them in the Word Search below.

WORD LIST

STATE	RIVER	PEOPLE	TREE	BIRD
FLAG	VOTE	FLOWER	SONG	OCEAN

```
A X N Y H N V S D G T R E P
V O T E M A C S E A B A Y E
S N B R X B R K S X B D S O
Y B P Q L S O N G R I J H P
R I V E R P P L R T Y U E L
Q R E R T Y Z E E R T O N E
R D P P A H A O N E C K A R
S X O C E A N C P W E R N I
P O B U Y U Y H E O L L D O
Q U F L A G R K R L X Z O P
Z X R D G H R E U F L L A L
M R D W Q N M N S T A T E Z
```

New Jersey
Trivia

I ♥ New Jersey!

The Netherlands owned New Jersey until it was ceded to the British in 1664.

Many New Jerseyans fought during World War II. Those left at home worked to supply food and other goods for the war. Some were held in internment camps. New Jerseyans also fought in the Vietnam War and the Gulf War.

New Jersey's state colors are buff and blue.

The first baseball game was played in Hoboken, New Jersey.

Saltwater taffy was first made and sold in New Jersey!

Charles E. Hires first developed root beer in Roadstown, New Jersey in 1876.

Vineland, New Jersey is the dandelion capital of the world.

Thomas Edison was called the Wizard of Menlo Park.

Bluefish are sometimes called Jersey Jumbos.

The oldest operating lighthouse in America has been shining in Sandy Hook since 1764.

Elizabeth White of New Jersey pioneered the cultivation and marketing of blueberries.

New Jersey
The 3rd State

Do you know when New Jersey became a state? New Jersey became the 3rd state in 1787.

Color New Jersey red. Color the Atlantic and the Pacific Ocean blue. Color the rest of the U.S. states shown here green.

Pacific Ocean

Atlantic Ocean

NJ

N
NW   NE
W   E
SW   SE
S

New Jersey
State Flag

The state flag of New Jersey was adopted in 1896. It shows the state seal centered on a gold background. The seal shows the state motto and the date, 1776, the year New Jersey signed the Declaration of Independence. As you travel throughout New Jersey, look for it on government buildings and vehicles!

Color the New Jersey flag below.

New Jersey State Bird

Most states have a state bird. It reminds us that we should "fly high" to achieve our goals. The state bird of New Jersey is the eastern goldfinch. It has yellow feathers and a black forehead and wings. The bird flies up and down like a roller coaster and sings a bright, clear song.

Circle your state bird, then color all the birds.

THE EARLY BIRD GETS THE WORM!

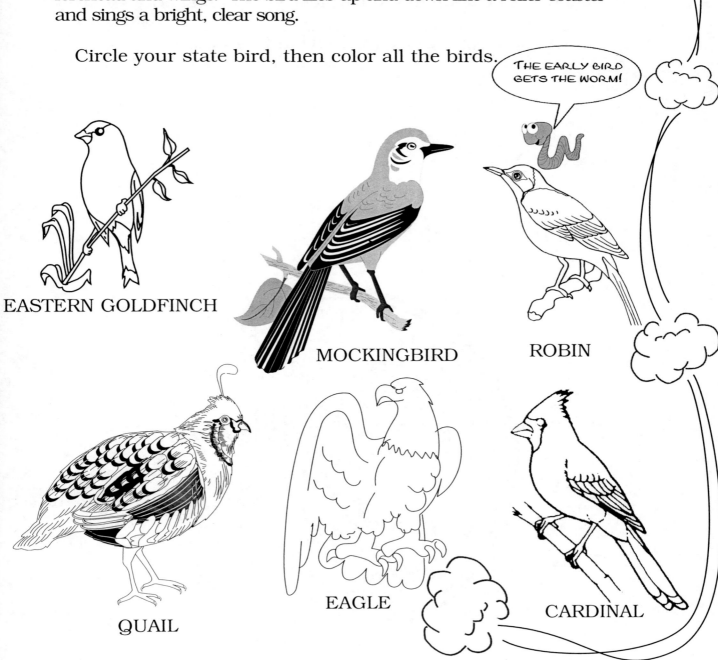

EASTERN GOLDFINCH

MOCKINGBIRD

ROBIN

QUAIL

EAGLE

CARDINAL

New Jersey
State Seal and Motto

The New Jersey state seal shows a shield with three plows, Liberty, the goddess Ceres, and the horn of plenty. In Roman mythology, Ceres, was an earth or agriculture goddess. The state motto is "Liberty and Prosperity."

In 25 words or less, explain what this means:

_____

_____

_____

_____

Color the state seal.

...WITH LIBERTY AND JUSTICE FOR ALL!

New Jersey
State Flower

Every state has a favorite flower. The common meadow violet, viola sororia, became the state flower in 1971. There are over 400 species of violets throughout the world. Violet petals can be candied and are sometimes used to make jelly. The leaves can be added to salads.

Color the picture of our state flower.

New Jersey
State Trees

Our state tree reminds us that our roots should run deep if we want to grow straight and tall! New Jersey's official state tree is the red oak. The fruit of the red oak is called an acorn. New Jersey's state memorial tree is the dogwood. Dogwood leaves are among the first to change color in the fall.

Finish drawing the trees, then color them.

Wow!

New Jersey
State Zoos

New Jersey has many zoos around the state. Some of them include the Cape May County Park, the Cohanzick Zoo, Popcorn Park Zoo, and the Turtle Back Zoo. Don't they have funny names?

Match the name of the zoo animal with its picture.

ZEBRA

GIRAFFE

MONKEY

BEAR

TIGER

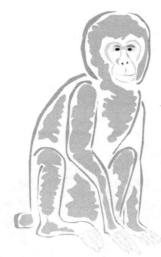

State Explorers

Henry Hudson and his crew were the first Europeans to set foot in New Jersey. They sailed from Holland under the direction of the East India Company. Hudson was searching for a way to sail from Europe to Asia.

At that time, they did not know how big North America really was. They sailed up a river which was later named the Hudson River in his honor. Since it didn't lead them to Asia, they turned around and went home.

Color the things an explorer might have used.

LET'S GO EXPLORING!

New Jersey
State Insect

Honeybee
apis mellifera

The honeybee was named the New Jersey state insect in 1974. Honeybees make their nests all over the state. They are called social bees because they live in colonies with a queen and thousands of worker bees.

Put an X by the insects that are <u>not</u> honeybees and then color all the critters!

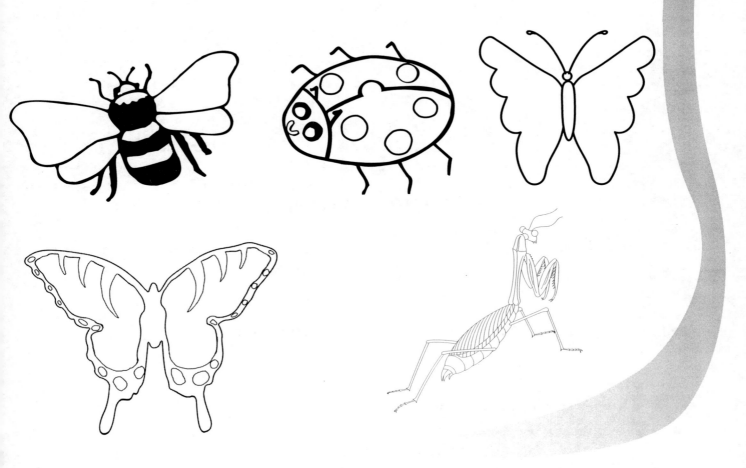

One Day I Can Vote!

When you are 18 and register according to state laws - you can vote! So please do! Your vote counts!

You are running for a class office.

You get 41 votes!

Here is your opponent!

He gets 16 votes!

ANSWER THE FOLLOWING QUESTIONS:

1. Who won? ❑ you ❑ your opponent

2. How many votes were cast altogether? ▭

3. How many votes did the winner win by? ▭

New Jersey
State Capital

In 1714, William Trent, a Philadelphia merchant, began laying out a town and offering lots for sale near the junction of Assunpink Creek and the Delaware River. The area became known as Trent's Town, and eventually, Trenton.

Trenton is the state capital of New Jersey. Add your hometown to the map. Now add other towns you have visited to the map.

(CHECK AND SEE IF YOU SPELLED THEM CORRECTLY!)

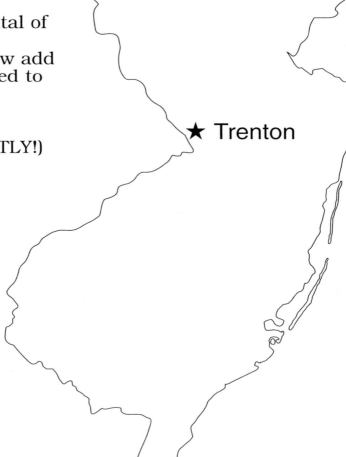

★ Trenton

Capital? Capitol? Which is which?

One word: Dictionary

New Jersey
Governor

The governor of New Jersey is our state's leader.
Do some research to complete the biography of our governor.

Governor's name:
_____

Paste a picture of the governor in
the box.

The governor was born in this
state:
_____

The governor has been in office since:
_____

Names of the governor's family members:
_____
_____
_____

Interesting facts about the governor:
_____
_____
_____
_____
_____
_____

New Jersey
Crops

Some families in our state make their living from the land. Some of our state's crops or agricultural products are:

WORD BANK

corn	blueberries	wheat
soybeans	cranberries	peaches

UNSCRAMBLE THESE IMPORTANT STATE CROPS

ahtwe _____   rnco _____

uesbberriel _____   ysnabose _____

ariesnbercr _____   ahepcse _____

New Jersey
State Holidays

These are some of the holidays that New Jersey celebrates. Number these holidays in order from the beginning of the year.

Columbus Day 2nd Monday in October	Thanksgiving 3rd Thursday in November	Presidents' Day 3rd Monday in February
Independence Day July 4	Labor Day first Monday in September	New Year's Day January 1
Memorial Day last Monday in May	Veterans Day November 11	Christmas December 25